Overcoming Obstacles:

Living With Congenital Hydrocephalus and its Disabilities

Overcoming Obstacles:

Living With Congenital Hydrocephalus and its Disabilities

By

Monifa Jones

Dedication

I dedicate my book to my dear mother, who has always been there for me through the good and bad times. I'm so grateful for her being there for my daughter financially, mentally, physically and emotionally, when I wasn't able to do so. I don't know what I would've done without her, as I've been on this single parent journey for eighteen years now!

Acknowledgements

To my sister Nefertiti: you've helped me in ways unimaginable! I could never repay you for all of the kind gestures and gifts you've given me! I will always be your nurse when you're not feeling well. I've got your back!

To my sister Felice: thanks for the long talks and laughter during the late night hours.

To my brother Keith: thanks for the positive words and for pushing me to finish my book, and for pushing me to tell my story of overcoming Hydrocephalus!

To my brother AJ: I was extremely touched to find out during the pumpkin run race, that you told one of your running buddies that every time you run, you run in honor of me!

To my baby brother Kashaka: I'm so proud of you and the man you've become! I still can't believe that you're a changed man! I still find myself staring at you, because you are a hardworking man now!

To my dad Clarence: who never treated me different because of my Hydrocephalus, and never left me out of any activities as a child growing up.

To my daughter Makayla: I'm so proud of the young woman you're becoming while staying focused on your schoolwork, as you work towards becoming a NICU doctor.

To my aunt Earline: thanks for rescuing me years ago! I don't know where I would be if you hadn't done so!

To my two aunts, Anner and Lizzie: I will always come and visit you guys as long as I'm able to.

To the rest of my family and friends: thanks for the positive feedback! My dream is about to come to fruition!

To Mrs. Cathy Levine: thanks for the listening ear when I needed to talk about all the ugly challenges I had faced over the course of the spring 2016 semester. I enjoyed the many lunches we had together.

To Miss Jackie: thanks for uplifting me when I was down and extremely frustrated at times. You've always said that I can do it, or "You'll get it done, keep going."

To Mr. Levi Frazier: You are brilliant when it comes to putting those stage plays together! You have a very creative mind. Thanks for the kind words after my "I'm Still Standing" piece at Mt. Vernon Baptist Church.

Table of Contents

Chapter 1: Unforeseen Circumstances: The Diagnosis

My father, Clarence Parron, is a native of Coretta, West Virginia. He was born October 8, 1945 but his birth certificate says the year was 1946. He and his siblings made up a clan of five, starting with him and his sister Charlotte and 3 other sisters. Because of financial difficulty, they were adopted by his aunt Georgina at early ages.

A graduate of McDowell County, West Virginia, my father was destined to start anew, away from the cold and shuffled life he lived as a young boy. During his journey, he ended up in the motor city: Detroit, Michigan where he met his first wife, Maxine. They dated for some time and eventually got married and conceived had two children: Felice, who is the oldest, then a year or so later, my brother Keith, was born. Their union lasted close to twenty-one years, but they filed for divorce on the grounds of irreconcilable differences. They remained close because of the children.

After the divorce, the young father of two decides to stay in Detroit and find a descent paying job to better provide for his children. He would soon find work as a painter. It didn't pay much in the beginning, but he was well on his way to having a financial increase! He worked for a while and saved up enough money to move into his own place.

Once he settled in, he met a beautiful, young woman named Betty Jones who had moved in next door. During the introduction, Betty discovered that Clarence was really into African culture, and he had given her an African name after they started dating a while. Birungi was her African name, and his African name was Gikuyu.

After a few months of dating, my then, 20 year old mother became pregnant with me. While carrying me, she was extremely healthy with no morning sickness and very active throughout her trimesters. She didn't gain a lot of weight (just normal baby weight) and there weren't any problems to arise. My mother carried me for the term of 36 weeks!

I was born November 13, 1973, four weeks premature at just over five pounds. I was fine for a little while, but about 3 months into my birth, I had become very ill. My mother told me when I had gotten older that I wasn't taking my bottle at all, but I wasn't crying a lot; I was doing a little bit of whining. My mother became concerned and took me to the doctor. She explained to the doctors what I had been going through as they examined me. My parents were told that I had a cold and I was given a prescription.

The next morning, my mom noticed that I wasn't getting any better when she witnessed vomiting and my lack of wanting to eat, so she took me to the emergency room. The doctors decided to run a battery of tests on me to see what was the problem.

My parents waited a while and then the doctor arrived with my test results. The tests revealed that I had suffered a brain hemorrhage, which is a type of stroke caused by an artery that burst in my brain. The hemorrhage killed some of my brain cells. Imagine becoming a 1st time mom at just 20 years old and receiving news that your precious newborn daughter suffered a stroke after being in the world for only 3 months! My parents were devastated! They also had learned that the doctors discovered that I developed a condition called Congenital Hydrocephalus (A condition where cerebral spinal fluid accumulates within the brain, typically in young children, which causes the head to become enlarged and sometimes causing brain damage.). My parents didn't know what to expect. My mom had began reading and educating herself to learn more about the disease. It had commonly been known as having "water on the brain."

My mom answered a series of questions that I had asked; she also felt that my head would be extremely enlarged. The neurosurgeons informed my parents that emergency surgery needed to be performed immediately to place a Ventriculoperitoneal Shunt (or V.P. Shunt shortened). It is brain surgery to treat excess cerebral spinal fluid in the cavities (ventricles) of the brain. A tube (catheter) is passed from the cavities of the head down to the abdomen to get rid of the excess cerebral spinal fluid or (CSF). My parents had to endure the plight of making the decision to have this major surgery given to their newborn! This was heart wrenching to say the least!

My mother didn't know how this illness would affect me mentally, physically, or emotionally, but the doctors explained to my parents that I had to have brain surgery throughout my life, unless a cure was found. Unfortunately, there is no cure for this condition.

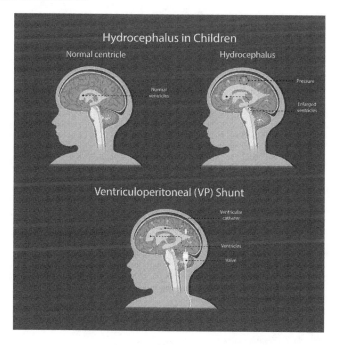

After my surgery, the doctors shared with my parents that they didn't know the extent of the damage done after the hemorrhage, but they would monitor me very closely to see how I was developing, but they assured my parents that I wasn't going to die, but depending on the damage done, I may be limited in the things that I would be able to do.

My mom said she couldn't remember if there were any precautionary measures given to my parents by the doctors before leaving the hospital except to watch me closely and to make sure that there wasn't any leakages. She made sure I didn't fall. She made sure she laid me on my left side because the incision was on the right side of my head. The neurosurgeons also stated that if I became irritable, if my eating habits changed, or if my behavior appeared abnormal, they were to bring me back to the E.R immediately! My mom was very protective of me, and she was afraid of the unknown.

My parents noticed that it took longer for me than an average baby to crawl, sit-up, and walk. But as far as talking, feeding and getting potty-trained, these were not delayed by my illness. According to my mother, I was taught how to feed myself at around 10 months old, and I was potty-trained at 15 months old; I had begun talking around 2 ½ to 3 years old; I started walking between 14 and 15 months, although I was walking on my toes, but nonetheless, I was walking. So my motor skills were fine.

As the years passed I was progressing greatly with just a few falls here and there. I had survived my first few years of life; despite the fact that doctors felt it would be a grave outcome. Look at God! Even though I was diagnosed with Congenital Hydrocephalus with a V.P. shunt, Cerebral Palsy, Scoliosis, Spina-bifida Chiari malformation, and Spastic Diplegia with a gait walk (which is a sway or rock when I walk), I was beating the odds! It was now 1978 and I was about to start kindergarten at Delano Elementary. My parents had uneasy thoughts about my starting school. Once I started going, I realized I loved school, and being around the other children was exciting to me. Although I enjoyed being with my sister and two brothers back home. It's just that the school experience was amazing to me! My teacher kept a watchful eye on me during every activity. I loved walking to and from school with my next door neighbors. My teacher treated me like a delicate flower but I was too young to understand why at the time. At recess, I wasn't allowed to play with the other children on the hard concrete. She always took a small box of toys to the playground for me to play with right beside her chair. Every day at recess I had to play by myself. It really didn't bother me. I just loved the fact of going to school every day. Everything was going smooth during my kindergarten year! Once school was out and I was moving on to 1st grade, I had wondered what it would be like. Would I have to sit beside another teacher without knowing why? Well, I was about to find out. As a 1st grader, I stood out! But it wouldn't be long before I was isolated once again. But this time instead of sitting beside the teacher at recess, I sat beside a new teacher named Mrs. Tarsy all day! And that included recess! She was nothing like my kindergarten teacher. She was firm! I mean really firm! I remember one time she didn't allow us to write below the line while writing out our words. If it happened, she would ball your paper up and say, "Start over! We do not write below the line in my class!" She would repeat that phrase several times during the day, enough to have my writing perfected instantly! I was so intimidated by Mrs. Tarsy's voice. She never talked in a soft tone! Even when she was being nice to the class, her voice was still firm. But she was an excellent teacher! As 1st grade came to a close, I was pretty sad because I loved going to school. But before it ended, I remember my teacher having a conference with my parents. In the conference, my teacher stated that she wanted to keep me for another year. I was heartbroken! I thought things were going pretty well, but my parents were being suggested that they consider leaving me for one more year. That extra year helped me to advance to the 2nd grade, but my twin siblings had caught up with me. So my parents had a 1st grader and three 2nd graders in school. We were all right there together but in different classrooms at Hamilton Elementary. I thought that that was so cool! My mother felt the need to explain to my teacher and classmates the condition I was undergoing with Hydrocephalus and the surgery I had years prior.

I was excited to be returning to school after having fun all summer long! My teacher exclaimed to my classmates that they were to be extremely careful about how they played around me and that as a class they were to help me out if needed. After a few weeks had gone by we had to take an eye exam. Of course I failed with flying colors, because my right eye was extremely crossed due to the trauma I'd suffered after birth. This led me to need glasses. I never liked glasses as a little kid growing up. They were always ugly to me! But I had to wear them every day. I didn't want to return to school wearing these ugly glasses! All I could do was cry! When I returned to school with the glasses on, the kids laughed at me but I didn't cry then. I just sat quiet that whole day. As a child, you never want to stand out amongst the other students; you just want to be treated the same. But that was never the case for me.

In the midst of it all, I was always going to the doctor for something. Whether it was for a CT Scan, which is an x-ray image using a form of tomography where a computer controls the motion of the x-ray source and detectors process the data, and produces the image to make sure my shunt was working still properly; for my Scoliosis, which is a curvature in the spine. I also needed braces to help me walk better, and to prevent me from falling more often than not. My 1st glimpse of these braces was scary! The shoes that the braces were set in were big and white! They were made of iron, and the doctor had stuck them in the holes in the side of some baby looking shoes. I had to put these shoes on my feet with the braces attached, and I was asked to stand by the doctor and walk. I couldn't lift my feet or my legs because these braces were very heavy on my little body. They were so heavy that I fell trying to take my 1st step. The doctor told my mother that I was to sleep in these braces every night and wear them to school. I kept falling as I was learning how to walk in them. I worried about what my classmates would think of me when they saw me in them. I was terrified! I walked in the school with my mom in these braces, looking real pretty. Every step I took, the braces made a clicking noise. I'm pretty sure my mom worried about me all day and how I was adjusting. I loved my new teacher, Mrs. Harris! She treated me like a gem or a precious jewel. Every morning when I entered the room, she would rush over and walk me to my desk.

My classmates always knew when I was coming because of the clicking sound my braces made when I walked! They would say, "Mrs. Harris, here comes Monifa with her baby shoes on!" It felt sort of like they were in awe of my so called "baby shoes." One person in particular always stood back and watched my classmates' fascination. Her name was Monique Jackson. She was always staring at me. Every morning she would look at me with a real stern look! Little did I know things were about to take a turn for the worst! My worst nightmare was right before me! Everyone she came across she had bullied, including me! Girls and boys, she bullied us all! Son, I would become her main focus! I will never forget the day she approached me. Her exact words to me were, "You think you pretty because you wear new clothes every day and the kids like you! I don't like you!" I couldn't respond or move at this point. I was just focused on trying not to fall in my braces. After I went home for the evening, I never told a soul about what'd happened to me that day!

Every day Monique would bully me! She would take my snack money and tablet every day. And afterwards she'd say, "If you tell anyone, I'm gonna beat you up!" So of course I never uttered a word! As bad as I wanted to tell Mrs. Harris, I didn't! I wanted to cry so badly! Every evening I came home from school without my tablet, my mom would ask me, "Where is your tablet, Monifa?" I'd tell her I didn't know. I couldn't bring myself to tell my mother what had been happening. So instead, I suffered the consequences and my mom spanked me for not having the tablet that she'd purchase every morning.

Those spankings became tiresome after a while. I knew I had to figure out something quick! But what?? Then it hit me. I had been watching my mother put on and take off my braces every morning and night before my bath. I mastered the concept and in realizing that I could use that to protect myself, I was finally ready to face Monique! So the next morning my mom got me up and dressed me for school. I was looking pretty as usual (my mother kept me in the prettiest clothes. I figured it was her way of making me feel good about myself) and my hair was combed neatly. Mrs. Harris greeted me as she always did, walking me to my seat safely. As I looked over at Monique, she wasn't too happy. She was always envious of me.

The morning was going pretty well until it was time for our 1st restroom break. Monique quickly jumps behind me in line and says to me, "You know I'm going beat you up when we go outside!" I didn't say a word, but I was terrified of what was about to happen! As we were approaching the restroom, my heart began beating at a fast pace. So when it was my turn to go into the restroom, I conjured up the idea to unbuckle my right brace since that was my stronger side and pulled my pretty pink pants down over my brace. Keep in mind even though my brace was unbuckled, I still had to pull my brace away from my shoe in order for my plan to work. So after leaving the restroom I was a bit relieved. As we walked quietly back to the classroom I didn't have any worries. Now it was time for recess. We were all lined up and ready to go to the playground and Monique ended up behind me. Again she says, "I'm going to beat you up when we get outside!" I was extremely terrified at this point! The walk to the playground was the longest walk ever! Now that we're outside, Monique takes my hand, walks me to the top of the hill and says, "What you gonna do??" Immediately my legs began to shake.

I grabbed Monique's hair and went in on her like a pit bull eating its prey! I was hitting Monique with all of my might! I then reached under my pants and pulled my brace off, whipping Monique's ass like nobody's business! All the kids on the playground began yelling, "A fight! A fight!"

So all of the teachers made their way to the top of the hill to break up the fight but they were unable to. I was filled with so much anger that it was extremely difficult for the teachers to tear me away from Monique. I continued to pull all of her hair out in spots! There were four teachers attempting to end that squabble and they still couldn't pull me off of her! We had to be taken to the office while still being attached to one another. Once in the office and separated, the principal questioned us about the fight! I was the first to speak. I stated that Monique had been bullying me taking my tablet and lunch money every day. Monique didn't have much to say when she was given the opportunity; no explanation as to why she was bullying me. After everything was discussed, Monique and I would be suspended from school for several days but before leaving, we were to apologize to each other. We each received a couple of days of out of school suspension. As we returned back to school, I wondered would Monique still be the mean bully that she had been before or not. Monique walks into the classroom but she wasn't quite herself. Something was different about her. She wasn't the mean girl she was before. Later that day Monique walks up to me and says, "You want to be friends?" I hesitated at first and I didn't say anything. Days had gone by and I approached Monique and said yes to our new friendship. No more bullying; we became best friends.

Chapter 2: Shunt Disconnection at the Cervical Level (aka The Neck Area)

There was a disconnection of my shunt at the cervical area (my neck area). It had been six years since my shunt had been placed in me. At nine years old, heading into the new school year and still wearing my leg braces, I had wondered what the third grade would bring me. Up until October 14th, 1983, I was doing quite well and there weren't any problems related to the surgery I received with the initial shunt placement. But that was about to change once the shunt failed to remain in place for the first time since I was a newborn.

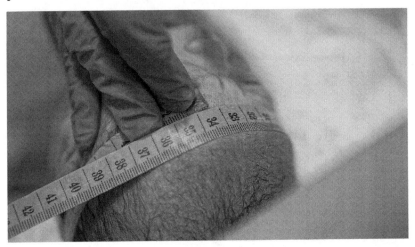

Six days prior to my admission at Lebonheur Children's Hospital, I had been vomiting uncontrollably for approximately 24 hours. Part of the reason why is because during the examination at the hospital it showed a disconnection and my pump had stopped working! I was immediately taken up to the operating room where neurosurgeons began prepping me for surgery and explaining to me what was about to happen. Afterwards, the anesthesiologist gives me a choice of fruits to choose from as the fragrance I'd inhale through my oxygen mask. The choices were: oranges, strawberries, or cherries. I'd always choose the strawberry flavor to sniff. Then the neurosurgeons asked me to count down from ten and I would fall asleep. After that I wouldn't remember a thing! The doctors began reconnecting my shunt. When I awoke from surgery, I could remember being in extreme pain! From there I was taken up to recovery. After the anesthesia wore off, I cried hysterically because of the extreme pain! This pain was the worst! Every time I moved I cried. The pain came from the fact that I had been cut in three different places: once in my neck area, twice in my abdominal area, and once on the right side of my head where my all of my hair had been shaven off. I was devastated! Imagine going from having a head full of hair to not having any! I cried and cried and cried! I felt so ugly! After I had this surgery, the doctors and nurses wasted no time getting me out of bed. They'd come in my room bright and early to get me out of bed to walk. I cried with every step. I had to walk down a long hall just to turn back and walk to my room. You talk about angry! This was the worst pain I'd ever felt in my life! My mom is the best though. After leaving the hospital and I was home and situated, my mom had gone out and bought me different color hats to wear once I returned to school. I couldn't go back to school until we went back to the doctor for the removal of my stitches at The Tennessee Crippled Children's Clinic in a month. I always hated the name of this clinic because the school children always referred to me as "crippled" or they would say, "Monifa, you're crippled!" The word alone just sounds so degrading. As I look back on this critical time during my childhood I remember seeing my first severe case of Hydrocephalus on a little white boy. He was confined to a wheelchair and as his mom wiped his mouth, as he couldn't control his saliva. I didn't realize at the time that I had the same condition. That image of seeing that little boy with severe Hydrocephalus never left my mind as a nine year old. Subsequently, I did well following that surgery.

For some reason or another, my little body kept rejecting these shunts, and I still didn't fully understand what was happening to me. I remember being sad a lot of times when I couldn't go home with my mom and my siblings after I had that surgery when they would come to visit me. I would cry often, still not understanding the depth of my situation. I felt like I LIVED in the hospital! It's October 30th and after being released to my home for a few days I was back at Lebonheur Hospital with my mom. Another distal shunt failure had occurred just 16 days after my surgery. There was a disconnection in my right supraclavicular area (or chest) but the doctors corrected this on the same day. Approximately 6 days following that, I needed to return back to the hospital for drainage of CSF fluid in my neck area. I was then placed on a drug called Dicloxacillin and my wound healed. It turned out that I had developed an infection in my chest and fluid began protruding through my chest. The doctors started tapping my shunt in the emergency room where I was once again admitted and wheeled up to the operating room. The neurosurgeons replaced my old distal catheter with a new one. Through it all, I had survived another surgery and on November 4, 1983 I was released to go home. My mom and I returned to the doctor 3 weeks later to make sure that I was healing properly. I have overcome a lot as I look back over that nine year old stage. After overcoming these obstacles and surviving several surgeries during the first years of my life, I'd say I'm extremely blessed!

I'm Still Standing

I'm still standing! Even after the news my parents received all those years ago about their precious baby girl who was diagnosed with Hydrocephalus!

I'm still standing! Even through poor eating habits, irritability, crying, and vomiting profusely; emergency surgery is what she needed at three months old

I'm still standing! Even though the doctors didn't know what the outcome would be; the waiting game began

Would she be a vegetable, never to do anything on her own? Or would she be confined to a wheelchair for the rest of her life, needing around the clock care?

I'm still standing! Your baby girl made it through surgery just fine; as the waiting game continued, my parents watched me closely

I'm still standing! The shunt worked well for 8 years

I'm still standing! Even through walking those elementary halls with braces on my legs as they helped me keep my balance

I'm still standing! Even after encountering a bully during my second grade year; she took my tablet and my lunch money each day that I entered the room

I'm still standing! Even after she threatened to beat me up at recess; she walked me to the top of the hill, only to receive the worst beating of her life

No more bullying; we became best friends and I stood tall in the end

I'm still standing! Even through going back to the operating room for another surgery; my little body had outgrown the shunt, which was clogged with fluids

I'm still standing! Despite my fear, my braces came off my third grade year; I was so excited to wear tennis shoes

I'm still standing! Walking tall like a ballerina on her toes moving forward

After all I've endured and overcame, my journey's just beginning, despite my pain

OVERCOMING OBSTACLES

My pains of society's ignorance because they're afraid to ask;
I'd rather you ask me than to whisper behind my back

We're not born ignorant; It's a learned behavior

My mission is to change society's way of thinking

I'm still standing!

Chapter 3: Isolation

August 7, 1989 and at the age of 15, my parents and I were right back at Lebonheur Children's Hospital, where neurosurgeons were prepping me yet again for another surgery. This was a stressful time for my parents, especially with having my younger sister and two brothers back home. My father had always been a great dad from the very moment we were born. He'd always take on outings throughout the city. The thing I loved most about my dad is that he never treated me different from my other siblings. But because I had so many doctors' appointments, my father stayed home most times to care for my siblings. Therefore my mom would take me to most of my appointments on the bus. I was always terrified of going to the doctors. I would scream, holler, and fight with each doctor visit. My mom would always make me feel better once the visit was over. She would take me to Shoney's, which was on the Mid America Mall at the time, to get a cheeseburger, fries, and a drink. I was much better after that. I remember this shunt revision well because this surgery was very traumatic. I was extremely sore and in a lot of pain. It was excruciating! I cried with every move I made. During this surgery, my abdominal cavity was opened and two incisions were made on the right side of my abdomen where my new shunt was placed. Gelofoam, which is basically a sponge, was placed to control my bleeding and to prevent my cerebral spinal fluid from leaking through my old shunt tract. Subsequently I was placed in the Lamar unit at the Myelodyspasia Clinic after this surgery. I remember the doctors working intensely with me in stretching my heel-cords to help make my feet flat to the ground. Evidence of paraparesis, which is partial paralysis of the lower limbs, showed in my left ankle down to my toes. I had always walked on my toes as a toddler, but nothing was done to correct it at the time. My mother came to visit me every week while I was in this facility. I can only remember my mom bringing my sister and brothers to visit me a couple of times. Every time my mom would have to leave, I would cry. I was extremely lonely at night. The doctors continued to stretch my heel-cords by putting casts on me every week at the Crippled Children's Clinic. And every time when the casts were supposed to come off I would scream and cry! The sound of the saw terrified me! This was the scariest time of my life! I can't remember how long I was in this facility, but my mom says with physical therapy and the doctors stretching my heel-cords, the treatment and therapy worked for a while. Eventually I was told that I began walking on my toes once I left the hospital. So I didn't have to be admitted back into the Lamar unit Myelodyplasia Clinic. For the next three years I continued to walk on my toes. I was now 18 and a senior in high school; new school and new surroundings. I finally made to my last year of high school. Here I am at this huge school and not knowing what the outcome would be. But I was determined to make the best out of my situation, because I practically lived in the hospital as child and young adult. It was October 27th, 1992 and a month after the start of my senior year, my shunt malfunctioned (it was a proximal malfunction, meaning from the point of attachment). I arrived at the hospital this time with progressive, severe headaches, nausea and vomiting. As soon as I arrived at the hospital in an ambulance, the doctors immediately examined me, sitting me upright on a bed in the emergency room. The neurosurgeons tapped my shunt with a small needle to relieve the pressure on my brain before taking me to the operating room where my Ventriculoperitoneal shunt was replaced with a new one. My shunt was pumping and refilling slowly over the next few seconds. I was discharged after my time in recovery on October 29, 1992 and nine days later I would return to Semmes Murphy Clinic to make sure my scars we're healing properly. I was doing well as expected.

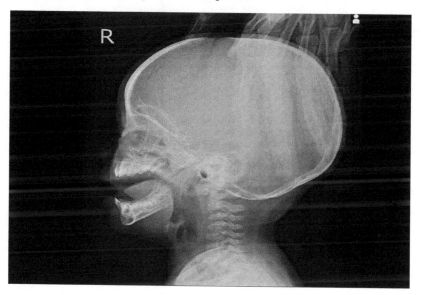

Chapter 4: My Sophomore of High School

My sophomore year at Hamilton High School in 1991, I was eager and very excited to find out what God had in store for me! The first day in homeroom was weird. I had noticed this guy staring at me from across the room. His eyes gazed at me for some time even as I looked away. Little did I know he had an agenda, I just didn't know what it was. Every morning when I entered homeroom, he would be staring at me. It felt kind of creepy! Within a couple of weeks he began speaking to me. He introduced himself as Shawn and I introduced myself as well. Afterwards he asked me if he could carry my books to class. Keep in mind I was still trying to figure out what his agenda was. Throughout the fall semester everything was going well for me. Heading into the spring semester I continued to get to know Shawn, still wondering what was his purpose in his attempts to pursue me. I still questioned to myself, why was he so interested in me? But the morning of February 5, 1992, I was going to find out. It was the typical routine of: homeroom, classes, and heading home. But this particular day was a little different. Shawn would usually walk me halfway home then turn back and catch the bus home. But this day, he lets me know that he wanted to date me. So I accepted his request and we began dating. Once we started, Shawn wanted to know what had happened to me. So I told him that I had suffered a brain hemorrhage after birth and it left me with in this state.

The relationship started off pretty well. Shawn was still his charming self; helping me out during the school day and what not. A few weeks into the relationship, Shawn's nice gestures started to fade. He started showing signs of aggressiveness. He was becoming more controlling and wanting to know my every move. It was at that moment that I had realized that I was trapped in an abusive relationship at only 16 years old. I thought to myself, "This can't be happening to me!" But it was! I remember the first incident like it was yesterday. I was at my locker getting my books for class, and who walks up out of nowhere yelling? Shawn! He yells, "Who are you talking to??!!" "What are you talking about??" I asked? Shawn didn't say a word. Next thing I know, he grabs me by my clothes and throws me up against the lockers, spits on me and walks away! All I could do was cry in silence because I couldn't believe what had just happened! Never before had I experienced something as awful and degrading in my life.

After I gathered my books, I had gone to the restroom to clean myself up before going to class. I was so humiliated and ashamed that I didn't tell a soul, not even my sister and brothers for that matter! The school day went on and I was still mindful of this horrible incident that had happened earlier that morning. I'd only been in the relationship for with Shawn several weeks now and I was already becoming overwhelmed with Shawn's out of control behavior! My relationship with Shawn became violent so quickly that I was afraid to turn back! Yes, I was trapped! I mean, Shawn didn't want me to talk to anyone, especially my male counterparts! At other times he would be so nice and charming as if nothing had ever happened. I thought that was crazy! But that was just his true character. Some days later, Shawn approached me at the locker saying he wanted to talk. I hadn't spoken to him since that incident; that left my soul paralyzed with fear and anger! But I couldn't free myself from this evil, vindictive young man! Shawn had a Dr. Jekyll and Mr. Hyde demeanor! One minute he was happy and the next minute he was enraged with anger!

I found out that Shawn was a heavy drinker, but that's still no excuse to put your hands on a woman or anyone for that matter! Shawn would come to school most days drunk, having several beers before homeroom. He would smell like a liquor distillery most mornings. I don't know how he functioned at all during the day. As sophomore year came to a close, I was trying to figure out how was I going to break free from Shawn. "How did I end up here?" I'd ask myself. I was crying out for help but no one could hear me. Nevertheless, during the summer, Shawn and I continued to date. On the weekends, his cousin Sandra would take us to the movies and out to eat from time to time. Even as Shawn and I spent most of our time together and going places, he continued to bully and threaten me with his violent behavior! Sandra would say to him, "Why are you doing this to her??" His reply was always, "Shut the hell up!!" But Sandra would always put him in his place! Sandra was pretty cool. She grew up in the heart of Memphis. She was very much a tomboy and she didn't play that shit! After a while, things would go back to normal. I had always wondered why Shawn was so angry all the time! I met Shawn's brother Caleb over those summer months. He was the older of the two. Caleb was nothing like Shawn. Caleb was charming, but he was respectful and he knew how to talk to people; two brothers who were total opposites from one another. After a few months I finally met Shawn and Caleb's trash talking father whom I will call "Jason." "Jason's" demeanor was extremely aggressive, angry, and disrespectful! That's where Shawn got his attitude from! "Jason" was cool as long as he wasn't drunk, just as Shawn. But if either of them had anything to drink, it was basically a done deal! They had no respect for women whatsoever! "Jason" was a hustler type of guy who sold drugs or other paraphernalia to make ends meet. Every time I saw Shawn's father, he would always have a can or bottle up to his mouth. Or in most cases he'd already be drunk. When "Jason" wasn't drinking, he was the coolest cat around! He cursed all of the time; bitch this, hoe that! Or his all-time favorite line, ol' funky ass bitch! He was the king of cursing and acting a fool!

All "Jason" did was belittle women and talk about their

clothing. By this time, my relationship with Shawn was so intense, I didn't know if I was going to live or die! I always asked myself, "How did I end up here??" I didn't come from an abusive home. My parents have always been loving and caring. They always provided for my siblings and I. I'm the oldest of my mom's four children. My father was married before and had two other children. So that makes me the third oldest of my dad's six children. My parents treated us all the same even when my other two siblings would come and visit us from Detroit, Michigan, which was pretty cool. It was the typical household. The only chores we had were to wash the dishes. We'd wash the dishes standing up on paint buckets. If you missed your turn, you had to wash the dishes for a week. It looked fun when my mom would wash the dishes so of course we wanted to try it, too. My baby brother would always miss his turn washing dishes and he'd get awakened out of his sleep between 5:30am and 6am to wash the dishes before leaving for school.

My junior year of high school was flowing well and my shunt was still functioning like it was supposed to. But my relationship with Shawn was very tumultuous at this point. Shawn had become more aggressive and more violent than ever! His abusive and out of control behavior was so bad that I believe some of the teachers feared him! I don't ever remember the faculty restraining him! Ever! I can only remember the dry-cleaning teacher coming to my defense once! He held him back as he was charging at me. He was pretty violent though to be so young. This was an ongoing thing with him. Once or twice a week he would go into these rages! The school administrators never did anything about it. All they would do from time to time was ask him to keep it down in the hallways. The fact that his mother Louise was never called to the school for his actions was still a mystery! Shawn was nothing like his mother. Louise's personality was funny. She was always bubbly and very talkative. She always treated me nice when I was over to visit and she would always fix me something to eat. Her tea was the best! I started noticing things occurring in Shawn's home that I didn't see in my home, like Shawn's disrespectful ways toward his mother by cursing at her or cursing her out. He would always display those temper tantrums with her and Louise would make him leave and he would later return that night.

Right after my senior year in high school began, I suffered another proximal shunt malfunction. I was highly upset because didn't want to miss school. Upon arriving at the hospital, I was experiencing extremely bad headaches and photophobia. The Emergency Medical Technicians checked me into the hospital and my shunt was immediately tapped, which means they would take a small needle and stick the top of my brain to relieve the pressure. What a way to start the beginning of my last year in school! I was not a happy camper! As I was being prepped and draped for another surgery, I had hoped I would return back to school in time to take Christmas pictures. I would have to take my pictures in a Santa hat because my hair was completely shaven on the right side from this surgery. Weeks later after going to the doctor and getting my stitches removed, I was able to return to school. I was back to myself in no time, making the grade and getting closer to my diploma. I really didn't care about the senior festivities, I was just excited to get to this point considering all I had gone through up to this point. Several months after my surgery my relationship with Shawn took an unexpected turn for the worst! Upon arriving to school that morning, something seemed extremely off! Everything was unusually quiet. Then it hit me, Shawn was nowhere to be found! That was strange because Shawn always showed up to homeroom. As the morning went on, I didn't think anything else of it and I went off to my classes. But I knew what this day was going to end up like. So who shows up to school at mid-day to school? Shawn! He was standing at my locker near the cleaning class. When I looked into his eyes all I could see was red! Shawn immediately starts cursing me out and talking about my clothes. I was every crippled, funky bitch, and any other nasty word known to mankind that morning! He was highly intoxicated and he could barely stand! He kept falling down drunk. I was terrified of what Shawn may do to me. He never got a chance to get at me that day because the teachers and faculty had finally intervened, and the police were called to the school. Shawn was arrested for public intoxication and drunkenness.

After all the chaos was over, Shawn's mother was called to the school, and the administration board had informed her that Shawn had been arrested for public intoxication and drunkenness. Shawn never returned to school after that. I don't know if his mom bonded him out of jail or what! A few days later everything went back to normal. Weeks had gone by and I hadn't heard anything from Shawn or Louise. Then one day out of the blue Louise calls me. She was calling to let me know that she had admitted Shawn into Lakeside Behavioral Institute. I guess Shawn's behavior had taken a toll on his mother also. Several weeks later, I received another call from Shawn's mother. She told me that Shawn's counselors felt that he was in a better mental state to where he could have me visit him. The following Saturday Louise picked me up from my house. She asked me was I o.k. I told her that I was. But I had mixed emotions about this whole ordeal. When we arrived, I noticed how tight the security was. We had to go through several checkpoints to get inside. Once inside the counselors talked to Louise and I for a bit before a female counselor took me to a small room, where I was to wait for her to return. After the counselor returns, she asked me questions about my relationship with Shawn and how it had been over the years. Apparently, these counselors had already talked to Shawn about our relationship. They made me feel like I was responsible for Shawn's out of control behavior when clearly I wasn't! I became confused! What had Shawn told these people? Afterwards the counselors took me into another room where I was to wait until they brought Shawn out. Once they bought Shawn out, we spoke to each other and took a seat. Seeing Shawn after all this time felt weird because he was so quiet. I had never seen him this way before! I asked him how was he doing and he said he was fine. But to me he just wasn't himself. I guess he was learning how to remain calm when communicating without all the vulgar language he had been used to. We continued to talk for a bit longer, but I still felt that I was being blamed for his out of control behavior.

I felt sorry for Shawn. He was in that place locked up with no way of getting out. But I was glad that I didn't have to deal with his abusive and controlling ways anymore. I cried because this was supposed to be an exciting time for as a senior, but I was dealing with what appeared to me a psycho of a young man. I had to put that ordeal behind me. But Louise was always in the back of my mind. No mom should ever have to put their child away because of behavioral issues. I could only imagine what Louise was feeling inside. I didn't say much on the ride home. Nothing was ever the same after that. Finally, June 1, 1993; graduation day was here! I thought I'd never see the day, despite the obstacles and challenges I had faced. Shawn's graduation happened inside of the facility along with other teens there. After graduation, I already knew what I wanted to do: go to college and pursue my dream of becoming a teacher, a writer, and a motivational speaker. Like most teenagers my age, I didn't start college right after high school. Three years had passed since graduation and Shawn and I decided to move in together. That was a big mistake! Things started out great in the beginning as Shawn and I settled into our apartment. Shawn was a hardworking man. If he were to get laid off from one job, he'd find another job instantly. After living together for several months, the past found its way back into my present, as Shawn's abusive ways had returned with a vengeance! I thought, "Dear God! Here we go again!" I thought I was past this point with Shawn. But no! I wasn't prepared at all. Any little thing would set Shawn off!

From my not answering the phone because I was busy doing other things around the house, to my not saying anything to him when he asked me a question. But that was just my way of keeping the peace within our home. Shawn was always confrontational, especially after a beer or two!

I remember one incident in particular. We had gone to the movies. Once the movies were over with, we went to eat at a restaurant to eat. As we were being seated, this random guy compliments me on my hair and how pretty it was. Shawn immediately went into this rage! He said, "You must be fucking that nigga, stupid bitch! You got me fucked up, dumb ass hoe!" That was pretty hurtful and degrading. Shawn apologizes during the course of our meal but I didn't say anything for the rest of the evening. But I cried uncontrollably! I literally wanted to die in that moment! I was so numb I couldn't even walk when it was time for us to leave the restaurant. On the way home, he asked me if I was o.k. and I still said nothing. I remember how I use to talk to God out loud. I would ask Him, "Why are You taking me through this hell with this angry evil soul of a man, God?" Shawn's soul was so torn and broken that it was beyond repair! All because Shawn witnessed his father "Jason" being abusive to his mom growing up as a child. After New Year's in 1997 my father had come to live with Shawn and I. It was pretty cool for the most part. No arguing, fighting, or bickering with Shawn for a while. Months after my father moved in, Shawn's Dr. Jekyll and Mr. Hyde ways was slowly returning! Shawn had started drinking with my dad one evening and I knew then what that was going to be like. Sure enough, Shawn had cursed me out for no reason! My dad was like, "Man, what's wrong??" Shawn didn't respond and went into another one of his rages! The altercation got ugly real quick! Shawn had always been the jealous type! I remember my father was sitting on the couch watching T.V. and Shawn comes out the room in a rage yelling and screaming, asking who had I been with? I said, "What are you talking about?" Immediately the argument became physical! We were fighting like cats and dogs! My dad tried to break up the fight but he couldn't. Shawn's hands were around my neck choking me! I screamed out, "God, please don't let me die!!!" The next thing I know, I flipped Shawn over and start beating his ass like nobody's business! Bite marks and bruises were everywhere! I was like a pit bull on his ass! My father tried to pull me off him but he couldn't. It was evident that Shawn's ways had taken a toll on me! Shawn makes his way into the kitchen and gets a gun out the kitchen cabinet and began waving it. He said, "Bitch, I'll kill you right in front of your dad!" It took my dad a while to get Shawn to put the gun down, but he eventually got him to. My father talked Shawn into leaving the apartment for a while. He left for a while, but he returned later that night. It was a long while before Shawn put his hands on me again. My father had been telling my mother about every incident between Shawn and I and I became upset and put him out! But I didn't realize that my father was only trying to protect me. I didn't speak to my father for some time after that. Eventually my father and I were on good terms again. My shunt continued to work well, despite my chaotic relationship. Through it all, I still managed to stay focus and keep my grades up while attending Southwest T.C.C.

It had been two years since my cousin Charles' passing. I still couldn't believe he was gone. As hard as I tried to put Charles passing behind me, it was hard to do because he had died so young. It was now August of 1999 and I had gone to the doctor for another check-up. I found out I was pregnant, but this pregnancy was short lived. I miscarried that same day while in the restroom at Southwest Community College. I was devastated! I never told Shawn about the miscarriage because he was the reason I miscarried in the 1st place. I felt that he didn't need to know because he was so damn evil! I was never the same after that. I felt that I was being punished by God because of an abortion I had years before. In March of 2000 I found out I was six weeks pregnant. I was in shock after receiving the news of my pregnancy from my doctor. I immediately told Shawn of my pregnancy after returning from the doctor in the rain. Surprisingly, my pregnancy was going well, considering that the doctors told me years before that I'll never be able to carry a child! A few months before I found out that I was pregnant, Shawn and I decided to move to Mill Creek Apartments. Three months into my pregnancy, Shawn's behavior was slowly returning. He had come home one evening drunk and began acting a fool. As I tried to remain calm because of my pregnancy, Shawn just kept at it! He'd began screaming, cursing, and began accusing me of cheating. Then Shawn pushed and hit me! As I turned trying to walk away from him he hits me in my left eye! My face swelled instantly! Then he starts apologizing. I was so upset that I started crying and I got my keys and left! I didn't know where I was going but I drove for hours. I ended up at Shawn's mother's house. I sat in the car for some time before I knocked on Louise's door. Louise immediately knew what had happened to me as soon as she looked at me! She called Shawn but he didn't answer. After I calmed down I explained to Louise what had happened.

Shawn's mother was highly upset! I decided to stay at Louise's house for a couple of days until I was better. I didn't want to face my mother right off because I was too ashamed. After a few days I was ready to go home. I could only imagine how my mom felt after seeing me standing there pregnant and with a black eye too. I decided to continue my pregnancy without Shawn. A few weeks later, Shawn began calling me but I never answered or returned his call. Day after day, Shawn would call and text my phone but I still wouldn't respond. I had often wondered what the end result of my pregnancy would be? Would my daughter develop Congenital Hydrocephalus as I did? That question was always in the back of my mind. But I did pretty well carrying my daughter Makayla. I had done well with my pregnancy until August 5, 2000. For some unknown reason my water broke while I was visiting my cousin. I was then taken to Methodist South, where nurses had examined me and from there I was transferred to Methodist University. Doctors and nurses began working on me immediately, hooking me up to all of these machines and wires. There were nurses and doctor's everywhere! It was so chaotic! Once the doctors and nurses were done getting me settled in, the chaos was soon over! Later, the doctors let me know that I would carry out the rest of my pregnancy in the hospital. Shawn didn't even come up to visit me!

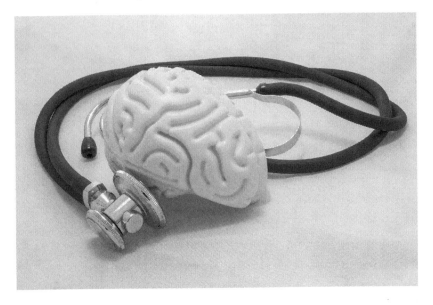

For the next 5 days, the hospital staff continued to watch me closely to make sure that I was in early labor! Apparently when my membranes ruptured, I lost a significant amount of fluid before Makayla's arrival. After being in the hospital for several days, I started experiencing abdominal pain. I called the nurse and she tells me that I'm in labor. I knew something was happening because I had never felt pain like this before! I called my mom. The nurse checks me again. I am now at 4 centimeters. Then I'm at 5 centimeters. Right before I jumped from 5 to 10 centimeters, my mom walks through the door and soon after my mom arrived, I had Makayla! A spontaneous birth is what I had! I was the talk of the hospital! After having Makayla, I didn't hear a cry so the doctors began working on

Makayla by doing C.P.R! Three rounds of C.P.R compressions and doctors had finally stabilized my baby. After Makayla was stabilized, she was taken to the N.I.C.U where she stayed for 7 weeks!

After those 7 weeks went by I was finally able to see my baby Makayla! She was born weighing two pounds and two ounces. I was in shock as I saw my baby girl for the 1st time. And I was even more in shock to see that Shawn actually showed up! I hadn't seen Shawn since I left him months ago. After seeing my baby girl for the first time I was overwhelmed! I had never seen a baby that tiny before! I let the nurse know that I wasn't going to be able to do this alone and they assured me that they would help me get through this ordeal! After talking to all the nurses and doctors, the grueling task of Shawn and I going back and forth to the hospital began. Shawn's behavior had seized for a little while. I guess he was pretty torn, too, after seeing our baby girl hooked up to all those wires. I worried that my baby girl wouldn't make it through the night because the doctors had told us that the first 24 hours were very critical! But as days turned into weeks, Makayla was thriving and gaining weight! My mom had come with me see Makayla. Makayla looked so pitiful and helpless as she lay there hooked up to all those wires. Every hour the nurses would call us to let Shawn and I know how our baby was progressing. I was afraid of receiving that dreadful phone call that our baby girl had passed! God works in mysterious ways as I knew He would! My prayers had been answered as I continued to pray for my baby girl. Soon Makayla was moved to an open crib and I was finally able to hold Makayla after weeks of going back and forth to the hospital!

Soon Makayla would be released from the hospital. She had mastered all there was to master; drinking her milk from her bottle as she learned the suck and swallow method, and urinating on a regular basis. Makayla was finally ready to go home and she was released on October 7, 2000, with a heart monitor in tow. She was born with hole in her heart, what is known as an Atrial Septal defect! Before leaving the hospital, Shawn and I had to be shown how to work her heart monitor. I was terrified! So for a short time I had moved back in with Shawn. I felt everything would be normal since we had a sick baby to take care of. Wouldn't you know it; Shawn was a natural at taking care of Makayla! But I had wondered when the irate Shawn would return. A week after being home with Makayla, she had trouble breathing during the night and her heart monitor went off. The question that had been in my mind for some time was, would I ever have to perform CPR on her? I had been CPR certified since the 10th grade. After checking on my daughter, she was in distress and struggling to breathe! I began doing CPR and Shawn dialed 911! The EMT'S made it to our apartment within minutes. Once the EMT'S had Makayla stabilized, Shawn and I were off to Methodist University, where the doctors and nurses checked Makayla over. Then the doctors came to talk to us. It was decided that Makayla would stay in the hospital for another week until she was better.

She did well upon her release. But once or twice a week, my mom and I were taking Makayla to the doctor to make sure she was developing properly. Considering the trauma after Makayla's birth she was doing great and I was thankful to say the least! Makayla was now approaching 3 months old and she continued to grow. She was becoming stronger and stronger every day. I kept wondering when the devil himself would emerge! Sure enough, Shawn's vulgar demeanor had surfaced once again. I always tried reasoning with Shawn but at this point nothing was working! I tried explaining to him that he didn't need to be fighting around our sick baby girl. Keep in mind since Makayla had arrived two months early, she slept most of the day! I became very concerned and I told the doctors at her next appointment. They explained to me that since she had arrived 2 months early, she was going to sleep like that because she's still supposed to be in my wound and still growing. Shawn had starting bickering and cursing as usual as he had come in from work. I had told him that Makayla had been in distress most of the day and that I wasn't for his bullshit! But of course he didn't care about that! As I looked into Shawn's eyes I could tell that he had been drinking heavily!

Shawn begins accusing me of sleeping around and he started cursing as usual. Then he rips my t-shirt in half leaving me basically in the nude, and started hitting and kicking with his steel-toed work boots! As I fell to the floor he hit me with his fist. But I got the upper hand and began hitting, scratching, and biting him while pulling his hair out! Then I broke our lamp over his head! He picked me up and threw me up against the wall punching me in my stomach. I became light headed and I fell to the floor. Makayla never made a sound during this awful altercation! Shawn and I fought for hours before he passed out on the couch! After checking on Makayla, I had gone into the restroom to clean myself up, because I had urinated on myself during the fight. While looking at myself in the mirror, I realized I was hurt really bad! I looked over my body, and it was covered in bruises! I was also in a lot of pain. I had gone back into the bedroom to lie down. Frustrated, angry and crying, I had become enraged! I had gone into the kitchen and got a knife! Then I went back into the living room and straddled Shawn while he was still passed out asleep. I put the knife under his chin then Shawn wakes up and asks me what was I doing? I said, "If you move motherfucker, I'm going to slit your throat!" Shawn began apologizing but I wasn't hearing any of that crap!

While still holding the knife to his throat, God spoke to me! "Don't do it, Monifa! He's not worth it!" I looked at Makayla in her carrier still asleep and I told Shawn, "Before I let some judge give you the rights to raise our daughter, I'm going to get off you and let you live, punk ass motherfucker!" I got off him and went into our bedroom, leaving Makayla in her seat beside Shawn near the couch. I pushed the dresser behind the door making sure Shawn wouldn't come in! I wasn't worried about our daughter because I knew Shawn wouldn't harm her.

After gathering my thoughts, I was still trying to figure out how I was going to leave this man! I thought about writing a letter to my aunt Earline. It wasn't that I wasn't able to talk to my mom, but it was just easier to talk to my aunt. As I began writing the letter, I started explaining that Shawn and I had been fighting for hours on end and that I needed to be rescued from this evil soul of a man. After I dropped Shawn off at work I had gone over my aunt's house. When I arrived, she was in the kitchen washing dishes. As I sat on the couch I let her know that I was leaving a letter on her dresser and I asked her not to read it until I was gone. She did as I had asked. Shawn knew nothing of my plans of leaving him. I knew once my aunt read the letter I knew I would be free and it was now a waiting game! That evening I picked Shawn up from work and he was back to himself. The next morning it was the same routine, but this time I dropped Shawn off at work for the last time.

That same morning I received a phone call from my father. He asked me to pick him up so he could help me move. I picked him up and we returned to my apartment to move our things to my mom's house as quickly as I could. That evening it was time for me to pick Shawn up from work but I never showed up. Shawn began calling my phone. I answered and he said, "Where are you? I'm off work." I said, "I'm not coming. Get home the best way you can." I had told my mom earlier that day that Shawn will be over here as soon as he gets off work for sure. And just like that Shawn shows up acting irate and ignorant! He started screaming and cursing both of us out! He told us that we had him fucked up, and that we weren't going to take his baby from him! My mom did things in a calm manner and never yelled or cursed Shawn. She continued to try and talk to Shawn but he became extremely angry by the second. This went on for hours. After a while Shawn finally left my mom's house and he never returned. Things were getting back to normal.

Makayla was still thriving and doing well at six months old. But after she turned six months she suffered a severe asthma attack! So Makayla needed to be administered breathing treatments. These treatments would last for hours. After leaving the hospital, Makayla was much better from taking the treatments. The doctors sent us home with an asthma machine and medicine.

Years would pass and Makayla hadn't shown any signs of having a disability or abnormalities. I was extremely grateful for the outcome of Makayla's birth after all of the trauma she had endured. Makayla was approaching a year old and this was a huge milestone for her. As for Shawn, he was back to his old self again. Later that year I decided to sit Shawn down so we could talk. I wanted him to be a part of his daughter's life because he was her father. I wanted us to co-parent and for Makayla to have both her parents in her life. So Shawn and I co-parented for a while, until Shawn decides he doesn't want to participate because I wouldn't date or move back in with him. Then he says, "If you leave me for good I will not help you with Makayla!" He had always threatened me with those words but I never thought he would go through with it since he had been a great father to Makayla. Even after we split for good he would pick her up from my mom's house, only to bring her back before her bedtime. He loved taking her to the park. It was her favorite place to go as a kid. Their bond was incredible! Every weekend Shawn would pick up Makayla and keep her the entire weekend. I was very grateful that her father was active in her life because my father was always in my life. As far back as I can remember I always said that if I became a mother, I would always make sure that the baby's father would be in the baby's life. But things don't always turn out as we plan. I chose to become a single parent because I refused to raise my daughter in an unstable home. The best decision I ever made was leaving Makayla's father. But I was very torn after this decision.

I Chose To Become A Single Mother

I chose to become a single mother to make a better life for my daughter!

I chose to become a single mother because love isn't supposed to hurt!

I chose to become a single mother because I knew that there was something further for me to achieve as a single mother!

I chose to become a single mother because he didn't want to be a father!

I chose to become a single mother because I didn't want her to see the violence that he bestowed upon her mother! I never told her why I left her father! She's 18 now; beautiful, smart, talented and witty!

I chose to become a single mother because I didn't want to do 20 years to life; life imprisonment without my daughter! I chose to become a single mother because I didn't want to receive another black eye from this monster!

I chose to become a single mother to show her that life doesn't end because of unforeseen circumstances!

Terrible circumstances that led me to a dark place! A place I thought I would never return from! God has a destiny for me! My destiny, my faith is to be able to tell my story of determination and motivation to succeed and not fail! My stumbling blocks became my building blocks for an extraordinary future!

Chapter 5: Shunt Malfunction

It's been ten years and my shunt had continued to work well up until January 13, 2002. Two years after I had my daughter, I had suffered another shunt malfunction. Every surgery was different. I had arrived at the hospital with severe headaches and blurred vision so a CT scan was done. My scans revealed a ventriculomegaly, or large ventricles in my brain. My entire shunt was to be replaced along with replacement of my distal tubing, which had been in place for 11 years. On top of that, I had developed a blood clot within the valve itself, which accounted for my shunt malfunction. I was awakened in the operating room in great condition, and there weren't any complications afterwards. Soon I went back to my normal activities. From the very beginning, my mom was by my side. I always wondered how she felt about this whole ordeal. Surgery after surgery and yet years later, there was still no cure for Congenital Hydrocephalus.

I was still in my right mind; able to do everything on my own for a year after my last surgery, and most of all I hadn't used any medical equipment in years. As far back as I can remember I had always used some form of medical equipment during my childhood: crutches, a walker and a wheelchair. These memories were not fun for me! The reason being was because I was always trying to do things by myself, even though I knew I was going to fall or lose my balance at some point, which I did often. But that never stopped me from trying. Every 2 to 5 years I would have another surgery. At 30 years old I had had multiple V.P. shunt revisions, never knowing what the future held for me! But I was always a fighter! I overcame challenges like learning how to walk, and only wearing my leg braces in my 2nd and 3rd grade years, to having surgeries throughout my childhood. I would certainly say I beat the odds despite what doctors told my parents years ago. Intravenous fluids, doctors and nurses were all I knew growing up as a child. I was faced with the same circumstances and procedures over and over. The malfunctioning of my shunts was a recurring event for me.

My 10 year class reunion was coming up and I was extremely happy and eager to see everyone after all this time! And Shawn and I were on great terms surprisingly! We had even decided to go to our class reunion together. The festivities were already set in place. The first night was the meet and greet! After arriving, Shawn's demeanor immediately changes. I thought, "Not again," because he starts showing signs of jealously as soon as I started interacting with my male classmates. As I continued to mingle, Shawn is standing with his back against the wall with an evil look on his face. My brother and some of our classmates noticed Shawn's disposition also, but they ignored him. I continued to mingle and my brother comes over and asks me, "What's wrong with Shawn?" I replied, "I don't know."

Shawn comes over and says, "You just gonna keep talking and hugging everyone like I'm not here?!" Then I said, "Shawn, this is a class reunion! And why are you acting a fool?" and I walked away. I knew then what the ride home would be like since I had to drop this fool off at home. As Shawn and I were leaving, I knew the devil himself was about to emerge! When the bickering began, I tried to ignore him but Shawn became extremely irate and starts cursing like a mad man!

After arriving at his mom's house, Shawn jumps out the car and runs around on the driver side and begins yelling, "Open the door, bitch! Open this motherfucking door!!" Shawn's mother comes outside and asks, "What is going on?? What is the problem?? I couldn't respond because I had all the windows rolled up, and this fool had lost his freaking mind!

Shawn begins kicking the car as hard as he could! I started screaming and crying hysterically because I thought he was going to kill me!

The whole time that Shawn was kicking and hitting my car, his mother stood in the yard watching. I guess she was in shock! She tried to calm Shawn down but she wasn't able to. Louise's neighbors were all outside watching as Shawn continued to kick the car and glass window. This went on for some time.

I guess one of Louise's neighbors had called the police because of all the commotion outside. The police asked Louise who was she and she replied, "I'm his mother!" I had called my friend Nikki and told her what was happening. She soon arrived to witness all the chaos, and I was still locked in the car. This fool still was irate with all these police around. Shawn didn't give a damn about the police being there! The police asked me to unlock the door but I wouldn't! They kept asking me over and over to open the door but I still wouldn't open the door! I rolled my window down and told the police, "When y'all apprehend this fool, I will open my door! Not before!"

Shawn continued his rant and the police had to get their billy clubs out; they threw him to the ground and handcuffed him so I opened my door. As for Shawn's mother, she was still in shock and at a loss for words as she watched the police take her son away. The chaos was finally over and Louise's neighbors had gone back in the house. With all that had happened, I had hoped that my shunt wouldn't malfunction again. It seemed evident that I would suffer a shunt malfunction sooner or later because of the unforeseen circumstances I'd endured with Shawn.

November 22, 2003, two weeks after my 30th birthday, I was finishing up my semester at Southwest T.C.C. I had just returned to school after collapsing the week before following blood pressure issues I was having. I had suffered another shunt malfunction when I arrived at Methodist Germantown Hospital. These headaches were associated with mild photophobia, which is a discomfort to my eyes because of the light. Once again, tests revealed clear evidence of ventricular dilatation. I was transferred to Methodist University Hospital and taken to the operating room where I was draped and prepped for yet another surgery. I already knew what was about to happen, so there was no need for me to be afraid.

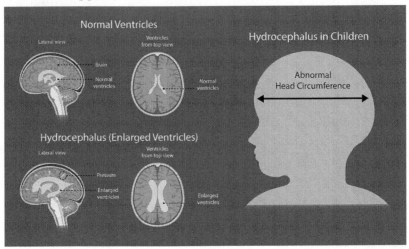

The operating room was always extremely cold! The nurses and doctors would pile warm blankets on me so I could stay warm, but that never helped! I was given general anesthesia and doctors intubated me. My head on the right side was partially shaven and several incisions were made so the neurologist could place my new shunt. Afterwards my head, neck, chest, and abdomen were scrubbed, prepped, and draped with betadine followed by alcohol. I was put to sleep by the anesthesiologist. Several incisions were made; specifically, one in the top of my head where my shunt was identified. Afterwards, the doctors repositioned my shunt and there was no evidence of CSF. The operation went well. I woke up in recovery after the surgery was complete. To the doctors surprise something had gone terribly wrong! They could tell when I awoke that I was disoriented! The nurse walks over and asked me a series of questions: Where was I? What's my name? Who was my mother? I had answered no to all these questions. The doctors and nurses knew immediately that something wasn't right! I had suffered some type of trauma during or after my surgery.

The doctors and nurses continued to watch me closely in case there was some sort of change but hours passed and there was still no change. I had suffered memory loss. I was also having trouble getting my words out. Not only that, I began stuttering too! I stayed overnight at the hospital and the next morning the neurosurgeons and doctors felt I was well enough to go home, even though my memory still hadn't returned. So on November 23rd, I was released. My mom took take of me to the best of her ability. I would ask my mom the same questions over and over again and she would say, "Monifa, you don't remember?" "Remember what?" "You just asked me that!" My mom also told me that I had begun stuttering really bad also. The worst part about this surgery was the fact that I didn't remember my own daughter who was 3 at the time. My niece, Kaneiqual who was 7 at the time, begged to see my shaven head! But I hesitated to let her see my head every time. One day I was standing in the mirror and in walk my niece asking the same question and again I said no! She then snatches my hospital cap off and I thought I was going to die after seeing my shaven head in the mirror! I screamed so loud that she had begun crying! I guess I had frightened her. This had to be a traumatizing time for my mother to watch me suffer on a daily basis, not knowing how long would the memory loss and stuttering lasts. A month later my mother returns to the doctor with me. As the doctor began his assessment on me, it was evident that my mom had lots of questions for him to answer. But first I had to get my staples removed. I don't know why staples were used instead of stitches. I was scared of getting these staples removed because I had never had staples before!

The doctor assured me that he'd be gentle in doing so. That was a lie! Right after he begins taking these staples out my abdominal area, I began crying! One by one the doctor snatches these staples out with no mercy whatsoever! I let him know that he was hurting me badly! He then moved to the right side of my head to remove the rest of these staples with these tiny pliers! I had become anxious and extremely upset all at once! But my mother felt I was exaggerating! I was in a lot of pain. Finally, the doctor had removed all my staples and it was time for us to head home. What a traumatizing experience this was! I now have a permanent dent in my head where the staples were snatched out. My mom continued to work with me, trying to help me regain my memory. I didn't even fully understand that I had a 3 year old daughter.

My mom never gave up on me! She continued working with me every day and she was determined to help me regain my memory! After a while, I slowly started coming around. I began remembering things that I couldn't remember before. Each day I got better and better. I know my mom was thankful for that! Soon, I had gained my memory completely! I'm sure my mom was extremely grateful for that! After fully regaining my memory, everything soon went back to normal. It was determined that Demerol was given to me either before or after surgery, and that I had an allergic reaction to the drug, causing my memory loss.

Chapter 6: Externalization of my Vertriculperitoneal Shunt

It's been five years since I had my last shunt revision and every time a new surgery date passed, I would celebrate that date anniversary. Whether I was going to my favorite restaurant, talking to strangers about my condition or just being thankful that I'd made it past another milestone, I had finally figured out how to deal with the public stares, the laughing, or even mimicking.

On May 7, 2008. I had gone to my PCP for my annual women's check-up and almost everything checked out well. As I'm waiting to leave, the doctor comes in and says, "I'm waiting on your last test results, Monifa." I was wondering what she had seen and if anything on the test was abnormal. I had been anxiously waiting to know what the doctors' findings were. My palms had begun to sweat and I became more and more nervous by the second. Finally the doctor walks back in and says, "Well Ms. Jones, I'm going to send you to take an ultrasound at the Flinn Clinic. I knew then she'd was very concerned about my test results.

The test revealed a 20cm x 20cm pseudocyst that caused drainage of a pseudocyst in my abdominal area. A pseudocyst is a fluid filled cavity resembling a cyst but lacking the wall of lining. A large pseudocyst that ruptures becomes infected or hemorrhages, requires drainage of the cyst cavity.

I had never heard of a shunt externalization before. Those words alone had my mind and heart racing. A neurologist came in to explain the entire process to me step by step of what to expect. He tells me that my shunt will be outside of my body and observed for 5 days because I had developed an infection in my pleura cavity, which is a narrow fluid filled space between the pleural membranes of the lungs and inner chest wall. My 9 day hospital stay was just the beginning. This wouldn't be a mere draining of my cyst and going home later days later. I had started crying once again.

So for five days the shunt that had been in my abdominal area since I was 3 months old was about to be removed and placed in my lungs. I cried hysterically but the neurosurgeons began reassuring me that I'll be fine. With Hydrocephalus, the shunt could be ran ten different ways. I thought I knew everything there was to know about Hydrocephalus; boy was I wrong!

After obtaining my consent I was taken to the operating room. I didn't feel sorry for myself at this point in my life at all, even though I have had several surgeries throughout my childhood. I was actually thankful because I knew my condition could be repaired by placing a new shunt. But I never really liked the idea of having brain surgery after brain surgery.

So, what is called a "time out" was performed immediately before the operation (this means that the nurses raised concern about protocol out into the surgical schedule of a hospital). Afterwards the neurosurgeons prepped me in standard fashion. The neurosurgeons made a horizontal incision under and on the side of my right breast, about 2 centimeters in length. My shunt was then pulled from my abdomen at the point of attachment but fluid couldn't be drained. I lost 3ml of blood during this surgery. My incision was closed using an interrupted 3.0 suture, and a distal catheter was sewn into my abdominal wall and connected to my external drainage. I had no complications after this surgery as the neurosurgeons transferred me back to the recovery room in stable condition.

On May 13, 2008, I had a CT guided fluid collection drainage performed once again on my right side where my lower quadrant was located. It was then draped and drained of approximately 2800ml of fluid was drained with no difficulties. I was ecstatic that everything went well with this surgery! That part of my surgery was over. The doctors let me rest up after leaving the recovery room, and they returned bright and early the next morning to take me back to the operating room to place my shunt in my lungs.

Luckily for me, I haven't had the entire right side of my head shaved since 2003. I practically remember each surgery and every time it was a different experience and outcome. My pleural cavity or my lungs would be the new home of my shunt for the next several years.

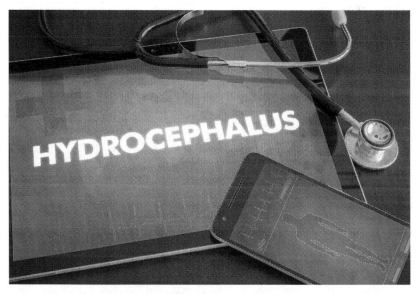

I don't take anything for granted. I'm so grateful that I've only had six brain surgeries thus far.

At 38 years old, it's been four years since my last shunt revision and I had been doing pretty well. With my ongoing battle living with hydrocephalous, it's never ending. Despite it all, though, I remained positive. The doctors and nurses were also surprised, too, because I was always upbeat smiling and happy.

But I remember being very upset and crying in the past at

times when I had to have another surgery. But as time passed and I understood my situation and the circumstances I was facing, I was okay with God and how He had created me to be.

The summer of 2012 was about to begin and I had returned to my home away from home, Methodist University for another Ventriculopleural shunt or VP shunt malfunction because of a defect in my diaphragm causing large abdominal pseudomeningocele cyst, which is an abnormal collection of cerebrospinal fluid (CSF) that communicates with CSF spaces around the brain and spinal cord.

The doctors were talking about running the shunt through the right atrium of my heart and again, the tears flowed heavily. I hadn't ever heard of this type of procedure up to this point. Imagine how I felt!

After the doctors explained to me in depth how these shunts worked and what was about to happen, I calmed down and I was okay with the idea, so I was ready to sign the consent papers. My medical papers also states that somewhere around the year 2010 I had developed an earlier pseudocyst on my abdomen and it was drained by interventional radiology, which consists of the radiology team numbing my right side with a large needle and draining me the fluid. I am awake during this procedure. The needle that was used was the biggest I've ever seen! As I'm lying on this table with these big bright lights, I'm watching as all this fluid was flowing off my abdomen like the Mississippi River! It was kind of exciting to see it happening and sounding like running bath water. But when my stomach was being stretched from this fluid, my abdomen muscles also stretch. So once all of the fluid was off my abdomen, my muscles had to contract and go back in place. I screamed real loud because of the pain, but I was okay after that. After about 5 minutes I was okay to sit up and I was released on the same day.

I had always paid close attention to my body. I studied my body like a test because of my ongoing issue from hydrocephalus.

Three weeks later I was back at Methodist University with the same issues, but radiology didn't drain me this time and I was extremely happy. I was having a few headaches but things resolved themselves. I had a routine follow up by my neurosurgeon, Dr. Stephanie Einhaus. She found another gigantic pseudocyst.

Dr. Einhaus discovered that there was a perforation (hole) or a defect in my diaphragm allowing my CSF to go into my abdomen rather than stay in my pleura or lung area; there was really not much of a pleural effusion at all, which is a buildup of fluid between the tissues that lined my lungs and chest. She decided that the best treatment was to remove the pleural shunt and place the catheter into my right atrium of my heart.

There weren't any headaches occurring and my ventricles had been slit three weeks before, which means I was experiencing chronic headaches; these headaches affect all people living with hydrocephalus. According to the Mosby Medical Dictionary, the characteristics include small ventricles and slow reflux of the valve mechanism of the shunt. I had no papilledema, which is a condition in which increased pressure in or around the brain causes the part of the optic nerve inside the eye to swell. Symptoms may be fleeting disturbances in vision headache, vomiting, or a combination of all three.

I was put under an anesthetic with respiratory gases passing through a tube to put me to sleep, and the neurologist placed a new shunt once again. My V.A. shunt catheter runs through my right atrium between my 7th and 8th rib.

A small portion of my hair was shaved on the right side. My platysma, which is a broad sheet of muscle fibers extending from my collarbone to my jaw was closed, and so was the incision made on my neck.

The anesthesia wore off after I returned to the recovery room. The next day I was able to get up and walk. The first thing I did was look in the mirror at the bandages on the right side of my neck, under the right breast area, and also the right side of my chest. Surprisingly, I wasn't in that much pain. After several days in the hospital, I was finally being released, and a week from my release I had to go see Dr. Einhaus to have my sutures or stitches removed.

As Dr. Einhaus removed my stitches, sadness and disappointment sat in really fast because the stitches had my neck swollen very big. I started crying because I didn't feel pretty at all. Why me? Why did God choose me to go through this experience? Every time I'd ask myself this question the tears would flow even harder. I had felt sorry for myself after I'd have my surgeries but it never lasted long.

I started realizing that these brain surgeries would always be a part of my life, unless a cure was found. My pain was short lived. I went back to my regular life and activities but I stayed in the mirror looking at my neck and it was so depressing. I cried every time I stood in the mirror.

Two weeks had gone by since that surgery and it was time for my two week check-up. I was a little better by then, but I was still a little down because of the swelling in my neck. Once in the doctors' office, I expressed my concerns with Dr. Einhaus about the incision that was made on my neck. My scar looked like it was bulging out of my neck; it was extremely ugly. Dr. Einhaus assured me that my scar would look better as time went on, and she was right. I was impressed about how my scars were healing.

Two years before this particular shunt malfunctioned, I had been under the care of Dr. Robert A. Sanford for 27 years. From the very beginning Dr. Sanford and I had an instant connection. Every time I had gone to see him, he would greet me with, "Hello, Monifa!" He would always tell me that I was destined for greatness! After being my neurologist for all those years, Dr. Sanford informs me that he was retiring but he never told me why. I was very emotional from the news. I didn't know who would be qualified to replace him, but he introduced me to his colleague, Stephanie Einhaus. He assures me that I would be in great hands. I had to return to Semmes Murphy Clinic and when I did, Dr. Einhaus informs me that Dr. Sanford had passed. I was devastated! As I processed the news of his death I would think of all the times he made me feel better after every procedure. I thought about Dr. Sanford often; I knew I would never hear his encouraging words again. I had to come to terms with his death.

UNTITLED

I had been under his care for 27 years. He made sure I would be o.k. even when I was scared!

Once a year I had to go in to see him. He looked into my eyes with this bright beam of light to make sure that there were no changes!

After that, he'd ask me to step down off the table just to see me walk barefoot on the cold, cold floor!

Once again I was asked to sit back on the table so he could tap my knees with a triangular object just to check my reflexes!

After that, he'd ask me questions to see how my memory was compared to my last visit!

After that, he'd press the right side of my head where my shunt had always been placed to see if the fluids would refill without stopping in its tracks!

If the fluids in my head were to stop along the way, I knew what that meant! More bright lights, doctors and nurses, and on the operating table, I went!

The surgery I would remember the most is the one of 2003! I remember the morning of November 22nd, to be exact because my daughter was only three! I walked into the kitchen to tell my mother it was time. "Time for what?" she said! "It's time to go to the hospital," I replied, as I began vomiting profusely!

Not a great outcome from that surgery; I was staring at strangers right in front of me! Repeating myself over and over as I tried to speak!

Three weeks in and my memory still hadn't returned! A couple of days later my mother returned to the doctor with me to find out that it was Demerol that had affected my memory!

I wrote this memoir in honor of Dr. Robert "Alex" Sanford! He was the greatest neurosurgeon to have ever lived! He always told me that I was destined for greatness; I will always remember our last conversation, which was about his retirement; he never told me why he was retiring; I know now that it was because of his cancer!

Doctors become ill, too; battling cancer, I never knew!

We had a bond like no other! I cried when he told me someone was taking his place! I was devastated!

He was 69 years old when he put me in the care of his colleague, Stephanie Einhaus, who also had a few years of successful brain surgeries under her belt! I was confident in his decision!

Chapter 7: First Encounter

Our first encounter was not in person. It was a simple phone call. He came off as an obnoxious, arrogant, and a rude individual. "Hello, how may I help you?" "I was purged from your class and I need your o.k. to get back in." In my mind, as he's speaking over the phone, I was saying to myself "I'm not taking no for an answer, not today!" Even though the phone call started off rough, as I was able to get back into his class, I found that he was actually a remarkable man, intelligent, and straight to the point! His knowledge and insight was amazing, and the quality of his voice carries throughout the room. As he began to speak, I knew within the first five minutes I had encountered someone of greatness! It's like an excerpt from an intense movie that you can't take your eyes off of! If you were to miss a class of his, you would have missed out on something inspiring for that day! The way he verbalizes his words is hilarious but meaningful at the same time. His pronunciation is like no other. You hear every syllable, consonant and vowel no matter what comes out of his mouth. It's amazing how much you can learn from one person in such a short length of time.

He dresses in bright colors, he often wears bow ties, and his shoe game is a wow factor! Yes he's killing the shoe game! Every class session was a mystery. He came off mean and rough around the edges from my first impression. But in actuality he was that teacher that expects greatness from everyone he encounters. He pushed me to heights that I never thought I could conquer as far as my writing and being able to stand before people to speak! Articulation is very important to him so there wasn't any half stepping for me! I always attempted to stay a couple steps ahead of him. If what he has requested has not been done correctly, he was certain to mark the papers with plenty of red circles!

People can enter your life for different reasons: whether to inspire you, tear you down as a human being, or take you to heights you never dreamed of! The wisdom he has as an individual is also amazing. He was my motivation to do better as an individual and as a single parent; to be that example for my daughter despite my setbacks, trials and tribulations. He has shown me what it truly means to lead by example. I admire his determination to have me strive for the best. If you want to succeed you must take the good with the bad and use it in a positive manner. This has been one of my greatest experiences ever, encountering someone of this magnitude! Expect the unexpected! He's full of energy, boisterous and stands firm when he speaks! The person whom I'm speaking about is none other than Mr. Michael D. Rounds.

It was a rainy Monday morning. I was excited about starting classes at S.W.T.C.C and I was eager to see what this semester would bring. I had registered for my classes right before the Christmas break of 2015 and I made sure to handle everything that was needed so I didn't worry about things at all. Before going to class, I went to the financial aid office to make sure everything was in place before starting the semester. To my surprise my classes had be dropped because my fees hadn't been paid. I knew then that it was going to be a long day. So I began the grueling task of trying to get back into the classes I'd originally signed up for and this was not easy. I started out at the Macon campus only to end up at the Union campus. Even though nothing had gotten accomplished, I refused to give up. I always wanted to be a motivational speaker. So what better way to start than in a speech class? I was determined to get in this speech class! I was back at the Macon campus walking in the rain when suddenly I fell. Some random guy helped me up and at this point I was so disgusted.

I ended up in the speech department on the Union campus where a lady named Mrs. Cathy was extremely helpful. After telling her what all I had gone through that day, she pulls up the speech classes on her computer and lets me know that there were 3 spaces left in one speech class. "Great!" I replied. She informs me that this professor was extremely tough. I replied, "He can't be any tougher than I am!" I was ready and willing to take on the challenge. Mrs. Cathy had gotten Mr. Rounds on the phone. "Hello, Mr. Rounds speaking." "Hi! My name is Monifa Jones and I was purged from your class and I need your o.k. to get back in." He says, "My class is full." I say to him, "Well I'm in the Speech department with Mrs. Cathy and she said you had 3 open spaces available, sir. After what I'd gone through today, I was not taking no for an answer, sir! Not today! From what I see, sir, your next class is on Wednesday."

Wednesday arrived and I got up, got dressed and I was on my way. I was extremely excited to see what the day would bring. As I entered the speech class I had hoped my name had been added to his roster. As Mr. Rounds begin calling the roll, he abruptly stops! I knew then he'd stopped at my name. He says, "This last name...Jones." "That's me, sir." I replied. "I'm the young lady you spoke to over the phone the other day." Mr. Rounds looks at me and says, "Since you insist on being in my class, Ms. Jones, I need you to give me a wow factor!" "Alright, I can do that!" With every assignment, it appeared that I wowed him! But those quizzes in the beginning were another story, especially coming from an E-Book, which I had never heard of. After I mastered this e-book, it was smooth sailing. Everything Mr. Rounds put in front of me, I aced it with no problem. The last speech we had to do before the semester ended was a farewell speech.

At the end of the semester we had to take Mr. Rounds' final exam. This consisted of thirteen chapters containing definitions. After class, I started studying to be ready for Mr. Rounds' exam. These chapters were a bit overwhelming. But I didn't stress over it because I knew I had made him proud as a student. The day of the exam we were all nervous! This was the toughest professor I had ever encountered. As we all walked into class that morning, Mr. Rounds asked all the ladies to put their purses on one table, and for everyone to turn off all cell phones and put them on a second table. He then seats everyone in different sections of the room. He sits me by the window by myself. He explains to the class that we were to open the manila folder in front of us after he counted down from five to one, and then we could begin.

When I opened my folder, instead of an exam there was a certificate saying I was exempt from his final exam! I was overjoyed and very proud of myself! I had given him what he asked for: a wow factor! I had done him proud! After the exam was over, Mr. Rounds said he wanted to talk to me. He informed me that I was one of his best students that he had had in a long time. I thanked him for the kind words. This was my final paper from this class:

Farewell Speech April 27, 2016

Today is a very emotional day for me. As I stand before my peers this morning, I would like to thank you all for this amazing experience. Embarking on this journey was the hardest thing that I've done in a long time. I have encountered a man of high caliber and excellence, and this has been a joy to me. His voice carries throughout the classroom and his spirit embraces my soul. To have lost his mother while still attending and teaching class, I admire him for that. The way he bounced back was amazing! To encounter his struggles and strengths is also amazing! His teaching has taken me to places I'd never gone before. I will always remember him as being strong willed, with the perseverance of succeeding at whatever he does.

To encounter a speech instructor such as you has been wonderful. Your views on life have made me look at myself in a different manner. Overcoming my stage freight has given me the strength and courage to speak before an audience and I am more confident in myself as a person. My most memorable moment is when I attended The Coffee House Production on the Macon Campus. To see the "Guy In The Glass" being performed right before my eyes was amazing! This man of greatness has shown me that life has no limitations. If you set the bar high for yourself you will never accept anything less. Nothing but the best is what I will strive for. There will be no half stepping for me because I know what he expects of me as a student. With his firm demeanor, he will be that teacher that I will always remember. This experience has taught me to never give up! Even if you receive some disappointing news from your doctor, keep going. Do you remember my condition I talked to you all about called Hydrocephalus and how it is a build-up of fluid on the abdomen and the brain? I recently found out that there is a small collection on my abdomen. Even with that, I still manage to have a positive outlook on life. I don't know if they're going to do surgery yet, but hopefully wherever this fluid is coming from, I hope it goes back to where it came from! That doesn't mean I won't continue to strive for my dreams of becoming a motivational speaker or an author. I know that there's a God Who has kept me thus far!

I feel that his teaching method is great. He's one of those great teachers' that's pushed me to the point of no return, because he wants me to be a great student. Surround yourself with positive people and positive thoughts. You create your own destiny and path.

After leaving Mr. Rounds' speech class, I was very proud of myself. I had finally overcome my fear of public speaking. After making it to my car, I saw that I had a message from Mr. Rounds. Here's what it said:

MO', YOU CAUGHT ME OFF GUARD TODAY. I HAD NO IDEA THAT I WOULD BE THE PERSON YOU WROTE ABOUT. YOU NEVER CEASE TO AMAZE ME! YOU ARE A WALKING TESTIMONY AND AN AWESOME WOMAN WITH A PLETHORA OF WISDOM AND KNOWLEDGE. THANKS FOR THE KIND WORDS. I HOPE I'VE MADE YOU JUST AS PROUD AS YOU'VE

MADE ME. I'M GLAD WE CROSSED PATHS AND YOU ENDED UP IN MY CLASS. YOU ARE A 4 FOOT TALL TOUGH COOKIE FULL OF INSPIRATION. #PROUDINSTRUCTOR

Weeks after I completed that speech class I received a phone call from Mr. Rounds. He had asked me if would I come and speak to his students. He stated that they needed a little inspiration from a former student. I didn't hesitate! This experience was indeed rewarding to say the least. I will forever be grateful for this phenomenal opportunity! When someone outside of your family recognizes your gift and pushes you to your limit, you must dig a little deeper to make your dream a reality. Since leaving this speech class I've been doing just that! Thanks for giving me the opportunity to share my journey with you Mr. Michael D. Rounds.

UNTITLED

As the students marched in and onto the stage the instructor begins to speak! "From Backpack to Briefcase" was the message he conveyed as the audience listened attentively!

His integrity alone is powerful! His honesty is brutal because he wants you to succeed as an individual and not fail!

The respect I have for this man I will carry with me for a lifetime! Every time he speaks I'm at a loss for words!

The compassion he has as a speech professor makes me strive even harder to become a first time author!

Punctuality could cost me my dream! A dream of mines that I know I can achieve if I work hard enough as I continue to move forward! Therefore I can't be late!

Teamwork is something you work on as a group. Most people fail at it because they refuse to work together as a team!

Enthusiasm comes from confidence, which is what I have in my soul! I surround myself with positive people, not worrying about what others think or say about me!

I'm accountable for all of my actions whether good or bad! My decisions determine the outcome of my future!

My opportunity came before me when I entered this speech class! The words he spoke were, "I can make it better for you, or you can make it worse for yourself by not doing my work! I made it better for myself and I was exempt from his final exam!

Do what you love because I love what I do, and that is inspiring people with my story of overcoming adversity and Hydrocephalus! For that alone I know I will rise to the top!

For better or worse I will continue to strive and do my best!

With that being said, I will tell myself: job well done! I have achieved my goal of becoming a first time author!

My essence of being a motivation to someone is to love you first before loving someone else!

I will achieve my goal by defining my Hydrocephalus as a gift and not feel sorry for how God created me to be! I want it bad enough to go after it! I believe it because speaking before people will inspire them! I've written it down so that I could see it every morning when I wake up!

I split my time up to make sure that everything is clean and organized! I read over my anger management pamphlets so I can remain focused!

I schedule my duties accordingly! I will make it happen as long as I have the strength to do it!

The illusion! If you think your career is going to fall into your lap, think again! You have to work hard at what you want in order to live a better life! This is my essence of being a motivation to someone else

Chapter 8: Unexplained Fluid Collection

It had been five years since I had my V.P. shunt converted to a V.A. Shunt. I was worried if my shunt would malfunction since it was now running through my heart. Would I endure the same symptoms as I always did? Only time will tell. These last couple of years in this phase of my life had been pretty interesting. I had begun feeling weird. Every night after I had gone to bed, I would feel pressure on my abdomen. Tossing and turning not being able to sleep, I would sit up in my bed. This feeling went on night after night. This turned into weeks, and weeks turned into months. I don't like to be in discomfort. I became concerned and I decided to make an appointment with my primary care physician. Upon arriving at the doctor's office, I had expressed concerns of the fullness and pressure on my abdomen at night. My doctor sends me to have an ultrasound. I had to wait days before receiving my results. The tests came back positive for an unknown fluid on my abdomen.

The doctor says, "I'm going to send you to Methodist University to have it drained through radiology. I checked into that hospital and admitted on October 29, 2017 where I would stay for the next 3 days. After having a CT scan done, it was determined that my V.A. shunt was still working properly. Other images revealed another pseudocyst had developed over time. The general surgery department recommended that I have an interventinal radiology guided drainage of my pseudocyst. This procedure was done on October 31, 2017. Soon after, this procedure was done, I was taken back to my room and I immediately felt better. I was discharged on November 1, 2017 and I was to return to Semmes Murphy

Clinic within 2 to 4 weeks to make sure this fluid hadn't returned.

It had been 6 months since I had that last pseudocyst drained but I was once again experiencing the same feeling as I did months back. I figured the fluid had come back, but I was in denial. I continued to ignore it and went about my daily routine. Every night though, that pressure was there. It felt like someone was pressing my stomach even harder this time. I made another appointment to see my PCP. Another ultrasound, another positive test for the fluid, and back to Methodist University to have this excess abdominal fluid drained. I was so overwhelmed! Frustrated and angry, I couldn't understand why doctors or neurology specialists couldn't figure out what and where this fluid was coming from! The great thing about this drainage is that I didn't have to stay overnight this time.

A year had passed since I had that last drainage done, and I'm doing as well as expected. But my walking was becoming worse after I had fallen in my apartment complex in the dark. I made an appointment to see my neurologist, Dr. Einhaus. I expressed my concerns to her and how I had been falling and she puts in an order to have a walker and a power wheelchair delivered to my home. I hadn't been on a walker since I was child. But I didn't care as long as it kept me from falling. Afterwards I began experiencing this excruciating pain in my buttocks area, causing me to fall even more. I am now in physical therapy 3 days a week for 6 weeks. It helps that I continue to do the therapy exercises at home. I feel like I'm starting to lose my mobility to walk on my own. But I'm a fighter, and I'll never give up! I am winning this battle against Hydrocephalus! I began writing poetry back in 2009 to express my pain and anger of society's ignorance of not knowing what people like myself go through on a daily basis living with Congenital Hydrocephalus.

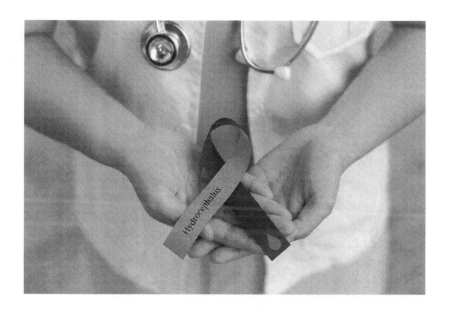

Chapter 9: Expressions of My Heart

I Was That Woman

I was that woman who thought she was in love! I was that woman being abused every day!

I was that woman who let this man take my spirit away! I was that woman who catered to this man! I was that woman who received a black eye while carrying his child!

I was that woman who didn't know if she would live or die!

I was that woman who hid the bruises! I was that woman who didn't believe in God! If there is a God, why was he taking me through this hell with this evil soul of a man?

I am that woman who found the strength to leave!

I am that woman who's been delivered from hell for 8 ½ years!

HYDROCEPHALUS

Having the strength that God's given me! Yearning to be that great speaker that's inside of me!

Driven because of my faith in God! Rejoicing because I am above ground and not in a grave! Occasionally I fall, only to get back up again!

Cautious as I walk this path of mine! Exceptionally gifted in more ways than one!

Praising God for bringing me this far! Having the strength that God's given to me!

Aligning my steps as I try not to fall!

Living a carefree life while here on Earth!

Uniquely created, I'm a Queen!

Sharing my gift while overcoming obstacles!

WHEELCHAIR

Willing to make a change to become a better me!

Hoping to inspire others!

Excelling along the way!

Evil eyes were always watching!

Living my life to its full potential!

Challenges I faced along the way!

Having the determination to continue on!

Always stayed positive despite my situation, even if it was difficult to go on!

Inquisitive minds always push themselves to the limit!

Reaching for the stars, I can never fail!

MOTHER

My motivation to be just like her!

Outstanding in more ways than one!

Thoughtful when it comes to other people!

Helpful in every way possible!

Exemplifies beauty!

Radiant, even when she's not in the same room as you!
Mother, that's what you mean to me!

FATHER

Furious because of society's ignorance!

Anxious to tell my story!

Traveling the world to educate others!

Having the courage to move mountains!

Exploring my options!

Revealing Hydrocephalus to the world!

DAUGHTER

Determined to do my best as your mother!

Always putting you first!

Undying love I have for you!

Going the extra mile to be there for you!

Having the strength God's given me to be there as your mother!

Teaching you as I walk this path of motherhood!

Extremely proud of the young lady you're becoming!

Reaching your goals without your father!

SISTERS

Sensational beauty queens of the Nile!

Inspirational in every way possible!

Shining bright like the stars above!

Touching the hearts and souls of the people around them!

Extremely aware of our gracious gifts as one beautifies the women of our great city, while the other one shares her gracious gift with the fitness world!

Renowned with illustrious reputation because of their many talents!

Sister Queen Nefertiti, the baddest beautician in Memphis! You and I rock out with all the giggles!

BROTHERS

Bravely strong and determined to succeed!

Rising above all others!

Outstanding in more ways than one!

Taking risks when they don't know the outcome!

Heroic men, my brothers, you are!

Excelling in everything they do!

Rising above all others!

Staying focused while moving forward!

Stepping Out On Faith

Today I took a huge risk and stepped out on faith to begin my motivational speaking journey!

A journey of mine I've always wondered about! What would the audience think? What questions would they have for me to answer?

To walk into the unknown; Hydrocephalus; my condition which is not a part of the outside world!

I hope to inspire people with my story! Stepping out on faith and letting the world know that just because you're faced with adversity doesn't mean that you can't achieve your dream!

Stepping out on faith as my mother did all those years ago when I started kindergarten! She dressed me in the prettiest clothes and my hair was combed neatly! She gave me the confidence to fit in with the norm!

Stepping out on faith! What is the norm? Is the norm trying to fit in? Or is the norm simply acceptance? I've accepted how God created me to be! Have you?

My mission as a motivational speaker is to educate the people! To inspire you as an individual; to encourage you as a person to strive for what you believe in; and shoot for the stars just as my mom did all those years ago when I started Kindergarten! She stepped out on faith!

MY WALK

My walk speaks volumes!

My walk is graceful!

I describe my walk as a God given strength that no one else can feel!

My walk is a special kind of walk! A walk that no one has ever experienced but me!

My walk is dangerous! My walk is fierce! Underneath my walk is my story; it will bring you to tears!

My walk is powerful; painful when I'm not moving! No prosthetics or crutches to help me stand firm when I'm speaking!

You will never know my pain unless you've walked in my shoes! One thing's for sure, I will not let my walk define me and keep me from achieving my goals and my dream!

MY SOUL

My soul was broken as a sophomore in high school! My parents never knew because I never told!

My soul was bruised, scarred and torn by this red haired guy I hadn't known that long!

My soul was controlled by his abusive words! I wanted to tell my parents but I feared they wouldn't love me the same!

I cried for years, 8 ½ to be exact! Listening to Gerald Levert's music was my way of escaping the pain!

March of 2000 I received the news of my pregnancy! Twenty

six years old, I couldn't believe what I was hearing!

Three months in, I received a black eye while carrying his child!

His mother stood by and watched him as he tried to kick the windows in on my car! She never tried to restrain him as this went on in her yard!

Sixteen years I've been gone from this monster, who is also my daughter's father!

DISCONNECTED

He's been away for 25 years, only to return home to a new world of unforeseen circumstances! Dementia on one hand and Parkinson's disease on the other!

Dementia: A chronic persistent disorder of the mental processes caused by a brain disease or an injury; memory disorders, personality changes and impaired reasoning!

To be confined and unable to leave when you want to because of your mother's ailing condition is the worst feeling of all!

Why me, God? Are You here to test my faith in You? Are You here to see if I'll crumble under these circumstances?

She's here physically! Her mind's fading fast! Tell me, God, when will it come to pass? I hate seeing her suffer day in and day out! I try and keep calm as my anger builds inside!

She's never treated me different even though I'm not her biological son! My dear mother, I'll be by your side until this battle is won! I refuse to be defeated!

My dear mother, I'll be by your side until this battle is won! I know that this is the reason that God had me to return home!

Home to watch over my mother in her last days of suffering! Just to see you this way is very overwhelming!

Overwhelming because I can't take your pain away! Not knowing is what scares me the most! It scares me because I don't know what to expect next!

Will I enter the room to find you on the floor? Or enter the room to find you sleeping peacefully with The Lord?

Parkinson's Disease

A chronic, progressive neurological disease! Marked by tremors, not my queen!

Resting muscle which God has bestowed upon her!

Watching her every move as he wonders what happened to her!

Rigidity, slowness of movement, impaired balance and a shuffling gait walk which causes her to fall! Paralysis! I don't know much about this condition at all!

Carrying her like an angel just to put her to bed!

Making sure she's comfortable as he fluffs the pillows under her head!

He sleeps with his door partially open just to make sure her words never go unspoken!

No More Suffering, No More Pain

No more suffering, no more pain; no more falling and getting bumps and bruises when I'm not home!

Watching you suffer tears me up inside because I can't find a cure for your illnesses!

Mom, you've always been there for me, even after dad died!

Now it's my turn! I put my life on hold just to take care of you! Just as you did when you adopted me and brought me home all those years ago!

No more suffering, no more pain! This is where God wants me to be! I will be here by your side until God calls for you!

Taking care of you is my priority now! I will make sure you're comfortable and feel no pain!

Chicken and dumplings for breakfast is what you want; I'll fix it for you, my Queen! Whatever your heart desires, I'll fix it for you, my Queen! Whatever your heart desires, I'll grant you your wish!

Eighty-five years young and you're still here! I'm so lucky to be your one and only King!

No more pain! No more pain! God has a new destiny awaiting you on the other side!

No more suffering from Dementia or Parkinson's! These chronic diseases have taken over your life! I know my God is gonna come for you soon and all will be well with eternity!

Your eternal life will bring me peace and my heart will slowly heal!

Heal so I can start anew on this beautiful Earth without you!

OBSTACLES

Obstacles will be before you whether good or bad! You fight the fight to be the best at whatever you do! Obstacles, I've faced so many! With God on my side, I made it through! The stares I've encountered on a daily basis just make me more confident in whom I am! Life is full of twists and turns whether it's unsteady or firm! Once I reach my goal, I'll tell myself job well done! Despite all the lows, I've overcome! In the midst of the storm, lightening seems to strike! I always knew that God would let me see the light! In my darkest hour I felt so alone but I knew God would bring me home! God was in the shadows waiting to rescue me! A place of having a peace of mind! I knew God would be there for me one last time! Standing tall with my head held high! I never had low self-esteem, regardless of who walked by! Despite the falls and battles I faced, God has always been with me, no matter time or place!

Obstacles! Know your own worth!

Everyone's Watching

Everyone's watching even when I'm not looking; the stares I feel when I pass them by.

Everyone's watching even when I'm not looking; thinking and wondering what happened to her?

Everyone's watching even when I'm not looking but I'm not worried about that because this is the way God created me to be; different from all you great people that surrounds me!

Everyone's watching even when I'm not looking! The whispers, the stares, that's what makes me who I am! To be that motivational speaker while inspiring other people! People of a different race or from a different part of the world!

My inspirational voice I hope to give to that little boy or girl! To let them know that just because you're different doesn't mean that you can't be great in this mean, dysfunctional world!

Everyone's watching even when I'm not looking! Wondering what I'm going to do next! Wondering if I'm going to explode with anger, which is what I've always done! I'm in a better place now with the hopes and dreams of leaving a great legacy behind me!

MY HOPE IS TO BECOME THE VOICE OF HYDROCEPHALUS HERE IN MEMPHIS, TENNESSEE. MY HOPE IS TO HELP PARENTS OF ALL RACES OVERCOME THIS CONDITION AND OBSTACLES THEY FACE AS THE HYDROCEPHALUS ASSOCIATION CONTINUE TO SEARCH FOR A CURE. I WOULD ALSO LIKE FOR THE PARENTS TO KNOW THAT JUST BECAUSE YOUR LOVED ONE HAS HYDROCEPHALUS AND DISABILITIES THAT DOESN'T MEAN THAT THEY CAN'T OVERCOME ADVERSITY AND ACHIEVE THEIR DREAMS.

I WANT OTHER PARENTS TO KNOW THAT YOU'RE NOT ALONE IN THIS FIGHT! I PRAY EVERYDAY THAT SCIENTISTS FIND A PERMANENT SOLUTION FOR HYDROCEPHALUS SO PEOPLE LIKE ME AND OTHER PARENTS OF CHILDREN WITH THIS CONDITION CAN LIVE A NORMAL LIFE.

MY MISSION IS TO EDUCATE YOU AS AN INDIVIDUAL WHO HAS OVERCOME MANY OBSTACLES, AS I CONTINUE TO WIN AGAINST HYDROCEPHALUS.

Philippians 4:13

"I can do all things through Christ which strengtheneth me." KJV

Made in United States
Orlando, FL
11 November 2023

38825288R00048